cookies and treats

simply delicious indulgent treats

First published in 2011

Parragon
Queen Street House
4 Queen Street
Bath
BA1 1HE UK

Copyright Parragon books Ltd 2011

ISBN: 978-1-4454-4048-4

Printed in China

The times given are an approximate guide only.
Preparation times differ according to the techniques used
by different people and the cooking times may also vary
from those given as a result of the type of oven used.
Optional ingredients, variations or serving suggestions
have not been included in the calculations.

Recipes using raw or very lightly cooked eggs should
be avoided by infants, the elderly, pregnant women
convalescents and anyone with a chronic condition.
Pregnant and breast-feeding women are advised to
avoid eating peanuts and peanut products. People with
nut allergies should be aware that some of the prepared
ingredients used in this book may contain nuts. Always
check the photography before use.

contents

introduction

The best regional food is known for its infinite variety – from *Boston Cream Pie* and *New York Cheesecake* to puffy *Southern Biscuits* and *Mississippi Mud Pie*. In this collection of recipes our sweet tooth is on display full force.

Here are classic cookies from *Chocolate Chip Cookies*, and sugar-y *Vanilla Hearts*, together with mouthwatering cakes, *Red Velvet Cake*, *Carrot Cake with Cream Cheese Frosting*, and *Pound Cake with Orange Glaze,* and pies for every occasion, *Apple Pie*, *Cherry Pie*, *Sweet Potato Pie*, *Pecan Pie*, and *Lemon Meringue Pie*. Included too are a variety of other desserts from *Homemade Vanilla Ice Cream with Chocolate Sauce* to *New York Cheesecake*, as well as breakfast treats, *Blueberry Pancakes*, *New Orleans French Toast*, and *Buttermilk Biscuits*.

Each recipe is coupled with a beautiful photograph that not only starts your mouth watering, but shows you just how beautiful your masterpiece will be. A perfect collection of all those "must-have" sweets for every occasion, whether it's a special birthday, a Thanksgiving dinner, a Christmas party, a Mother's Day breakfast-in-bed, or a July 4th. picnic. All the recipes are complete and delicious, yet, thankfully, are as easy as pie.

cookies and bars

chocolate chip cookies

A well-made chocolate chip cookie is about as close to perfection as you'll ever get.

makes 30 cookies

2¼ cups all-purpose flour

1 teaspoon baking soda

1 teaspoon salt

1 cup (2 sticks) butter, room temperature

¾ cup firmly packed light brown sugar

¾ cup sugar

1 teaspoon vanilla extract

2 large eggs

2 cups semisweet chocolate chips

1 cup chopped walnuts, optional

Preheat oven to 375°F. Add the flour, baking soda, and salt to a small mixing bowl. Whisk together briefly to combine. In another bowl, use an electric mixer to beat the butter, brown sugar, white granulated sugar, and vanilla extract until light and creamy.

Add eggs one at a time, beating thoroughly after each addition. Stir in the flour mixture until combined. Stir in the chocolate chips and nuts, if using. Drop the cookie dough by rounded tablespoons on ungreased baking sheets about 3 inches apart.

Bake for about 10 minutes, or until lightly browned around the edges. Let sit on the baking sheets for 2 minutes, and then remove to wire cooling racks.

peanut butter cookies

You know that feeling when you're really craving "something" good, but can't decide what that "something" is? It's these melt-in-your-mouth peanut butter cookies.

makes 12-15 cookies

1½ **cups all-purpose flour**

½ **teaspoon baking powder**

½ **teaspoon salt**

1 **cup creamy peanut butter**

½ **cup (1 stick) butter, room temperature**

1¼ **teaspoons vanilla extract**

½ **cup firmly packed light brown sugar**

½ **cup sugar**

2 **eggs**

Preheat oven to 350°F. Sift together the flour, baking powder, and salt in a mixing bowl; reserve. In a large mixing bowl, cream the peanut butter, butter, and vanilla together until smooth. Add the sugars, and cream for one more minute. Mix in the eggs one at a time. Mix in the flour, half at a time.

Wrap the dough in plastic wrap and refrigerate for at least 2 hours. Once chilled, roll or scoop the dough into 1½-inch balls, and place 3 inches apart on an ungreased or silicon-lined baking sheet.

Use a fork to flatten each ball by making a crisscross pattern. Bake for 15 minutes or until golden. Remove cookies from oven, and let cool on the baking sheet for 5 minutes. Transfer to a cooling rack with a spatula, and allow to cool to at least warm before serving.

chocolate walnut fudge

Contrary to what you might have heard, chocolate fudge is not hard to make. This easy recipe produces rich, smooth fudge every time.

makes 36 pieces

1½ **cups sugar**

1 **(7-ounce) jar marshmallow crème**

²⁄₃ **cup evaporated milk**

3 **tablespoons butter**

¼ **teaspoon salt**

1½ **cups milk chocolate chips**

1½ **cups semisweet chocolate chips**

½ **cup chopped walnuts, optional**

1 **teaspoon vanilla extract**

2 **teaspoons cocoa, optional**

Line an 8x8-inch pan with foil, and set aside. Add the sugar, marshmallow crème, evaporated milk, butter, and salt to a large, heavy-bottomed saucepan; place over medium heat. Cook, stirring, until the mixture begins to boil. When it begins to boil, set a timer for exactly 6 minutes. Stir constantly until the timer rings.

Turn off heat, and add in the chocolate chips. Stir until the chocolate is melted, then add the walnuts and vanilla. Pour into the pan, and spread evenly. Cover and refrigerate until firm. Dust with cocoa if desired, cut into 36 squares.

double fudge brownies

If you like dry, cake-like brownies, this recipe isn't for you.
These are moist, fudgy, and very chocolaty.

makes 9 brownies

1¹/₃ **cups bittersweet baking chocolate, broken or chopped into small pieces**

¹/₃ **cup butter, sliced into pieces**

1 **cup sugar**

¼ **teaspoon salt**

2 **tablespoons water**

2 **large eggs**

1 **teaspoon vanilla extract**

¾ **cup all-purpose flour**

½ **cup chopped walnuts, optional**

Preheat oven to 325°F. Place the chocolate, butter, sugar, salt, and water in small saucepan over a very low flame. Heat, stirring often, until the chocolate and butter are melted.

Pour into a mixing bowl. Stir in the eggs, one at a time. Stir in the vanilla extract. Stir in the flour. Stir in the nuts, if using.

Pour into a lightly greased 8 inch-square baking dish.

Bake for 35 minutes. Cool completely before cutting into 9 squares.

black and white brownies

These black-and-white bars are as delicious as they are unusual!
A sophisticated version of traditional brownies.

makes 24 bars

½ cup (1 stick) butter

2 cups semisweet chocolate pieces

For the cream cheese mix

6 tablespoons butter

8 ounces cream cheese

¾ cups sugar

3 eggs

3 tablespoons flour

1 tablespoon vanilla extract

For the chocolate mix

6 eggs

2¼ cups sugar

1½ cups flour

1½ teaspoons baking powder

1½ teaspoons salt

1½ tablespoons vanilla extract

1 teaspoon almond extract

Preheat oven to 350°F. Slowly melt the butter and the chocolate in a glass bowl placed over a pan of gently simmering water. Mix well and set aside to cool.

With a whip attachment make the cream cheese mix. Cream the butter, then add the cream cheese and sugar, and beat until fluffy. Add in the eggs, then the flour, and the vanilla extract.

In a separate bowl make the chocolate mix. Whip the eggs and sugar until fluffy. Stir together the flour, baking powder, salt, and mix into egg mixture. Finally mix in the melted chocolate and butter, and the vanilla and almond extract.

In a 9x13-inch pan, lined with parchment, spread half the chocolate mixture. Spread the cream cheese layer over that to cover, then spoon the remaining chocolate batter on the top. Swirl the mixture with a knife to create a marbled effect.

Bake for 40 minutes. Cool and cut into bars.

butterscotch blondies

Bored with brownies? What better alternative than moist and tender butterscotch blondies?

makes 9 blondies

1 cup all-purpose flour

¹/₈ **teaspoon baking soda**

½ **teaspoon baking powder**

¼ **teaspoon salt**

½ **cup (1 stick) butter, melted**

¾ **cup firmly packed light brown sugar**

¼ **cup sugar**

1 **large egg plus 1 egg yolk, beaten together**

1 **teaspoon vanilla extract**

½ **cup butterscotch chips**

¼ **cup milk chocolate chips**

¼ **cup chopped dry-roasted cashews**

Preheat oven to 350°F. In a large bowl combine the flour, baking soda, baking powder, and salt to a mixing bowl. Stir with a whisk to combine. Reserve.

In another large mixing bowl, whisk together the melted butter and sugars until combined. Add the eggs and vanilla, and stir to combine. Switch to a wooden spoon and stir in the flour mixture. Fold in the butterscotch chips, chocolate chips, and cashews.

With a spatula, scrape the batter into a lightly greased 8x8-inch pan or glass baking dish. Smooth to distribute evenly. Bake for about 35 minutes, or until the top is golden brown and a tester inserted in the center comes out clean.

Cool before cutting into 9 bars.

cinnamon raisin bars

Here's a spicy and new-fashioned variation on an old-fashioned oatmeal cookie.

makes 24 bars

½ cup (1 stick) butter, softened

1 cup firmly packed light brown sugar

1½ cups all-purpose flour

1 egg

1½ cups quick-cooking oats

½ teaspoon baking soda

½ teaspoon salt

2 tablespoons water

For the raisin filling

¼ cup sugar

1 teaspoon. cinnamon

1 tablespoon cornstarch

1 cup water

2 cups raisins

For the icing

1 cup confectioners' sugar

¼ teaspoon ground cinnamon

1 tablespoon milk

Preheat oven to 350°F. In a mixing bowl, cream the butter and brown sugar. In another bowl combine the flour, egg, oats, baking soda, and salt; add to the creamed mixture with the water. Beat until crumbly. Press half the oat mixture firmly into a greased 13x9x2-inch baking pan; set the remaining oat mixture aside.

To make the filling: In a saucepan, combine the sugar, cinnamon, cornstarch and water until smooth; stir in raisins. Cook and stir over medium heat until thick and bubbly. Cool to room temperature; spread over crust. Top with reserved oat mixture and pat down.

Bake for 30 to 35 minutes or until golden brown. Cool on a wire rack.

For an extra sweet topping add a drizzle of icing.

To make the icing: In a small bowl, combine confectioners' sugar and cinnamon; stir in enough milk to reach drizzling consistency. Drizzle over the bars. Cut into about 24 bars and store in an airtight container.

chocolate and oat bars

Two perennial favorites—chocolate chip cookies and oatmeal cookies—combined into one blissfully decadent bar!

makes 24 bars

1 cup all-purpose flour

1 cup quick cooking oats

¾ cup firmly packed light brown sugar

½ cup (1 stick) butter, softened

1 (14-ounce) can sweetened condensed milk

½ teaspoon vanilla extract

1 cup chopped nuts

1 cup milk chocolate chips

Preheat oven to 350°F. In large bowl, combine the flour, oats, sugar, and butter; mix well. Reserve ½ cup of the oat mixture; press the remainder on the bottom of a 13x9-inch baking pan. Bake for 10 minutes.

Combine the sweetened condensed milk and the vanilla extract, and pour evenly over the crust. Sprinkle with the nuts and chocolate chips. Top with the remaining oat mixture; press down firmly. Bake for 25 to 30 minutes or until lightly browned. Cool. Cut into about 24 bars and store in an airtight container.

vanilla hearts

Nothing makes a heart grow fonder than
a beautiful sugar cookie!

makes 12 cookies

**1½ cups all-purpose flour,
plus extra for dusting**

**¾ cup (1½ sticks) butter,
cut into small pieces, plus
extra for greasing**

**1 cup sugar, plus extra
for dusting**

1 teaspoon vanilla extract

Preheat the oven to 350°F. Lightly grease a baking sheet.

Sift the flour into a large bowl. Add the butter and rub it
in with your fingertips until the mixture resembles fine
breadcrumbs. Stir in the sugar and vanilla extract and
mix together to form a firm dough.

Roll out the dough on a lightly floured surface to a thickness
of ½ inch. Stamp out 12 hearts with a heart-shaped cookie
cutter measuring 2-inches across. Arrange the hearts on the
prepared baking sheet.

Bake for 15 to 20 minutes, or until just colored at the edges.
Transfer to a wire rack and let cool completely. Dust with a
little sugar just before serving.

cakes and muffins

pumpkin sandwich cake

A simple yet impressive cake perfect for a mid afternoon treat. Moist and spicy it's guaranteed this cake won't last long once you've tasted a bite.

serves 8-10

¾ **cup all-purpose flour**

1½ **teaspoons pumpkin pie spice**

1 **teaspoon baking powder**

¼ **teaspoon salt**

3 **eggs**

1 **cup sugar**

¼ **cup canned pumpkin**

Filling

½ **cup whipping cream**

½ **cup cream cheese**

½ **cup confectioners' sugar**

Frosting

½ **cup whipping cream**

1 **cup bittersweet chocolate pieces**

Preheat oven to 375°F.

Grease two 8-inch round cake pans and line with parchment paper. To make the batter. In a large bowl combine the flour, pumpkin pie spice, baking powder and salt; set aside.

In second bowl beat the eggs and sugar with an electric mixer until thick. Then add in the pumpkin. Finally add the flour mixture and beat just until combined. Spread the cake batter into the prepared pans. Bake for 16–18 minutes, or until a wooden pick inserted into the center comes out clean. Cool the cakes in the pan for 10 minutes before removing. To make the filling: In a mixing bowl beat the whipping cream to soft peaks and set aside. In a second mixing bowl beat the cream cheese until smooth and then add the powdered sugar. Fold the cream cheese mixture into the whipped cream mixture.

To assemble: place one cake layer on serving platter. Spread the filling evenly over the bottom cake layer. Top with the second cake layer.

For the frosting: In small saucepan bring the whipping cream to just boiling over medium–high heat. Remove from the heat. Pour over chocolate pieces in medium bowl. Do not stir. Let stand 5 minutes. Then stir until smooth. Cool for 15 minutes before spreading over top and sides of the cake. Finally sprinkle lightly with pumpkin pie spice or confectioners sugar.

red velvet cake

This is one of the few recipes where it's completely acceptable, if not mandatory, to use food coloring. Some older recipes actually call for beets to give this southern staple its signature color. As delicious as a "beet-infused cake" sounds, we'll just stick with a natural red dye.

serves 12

1 cup (2 sticks) unsalted butter, plus extra for greasing

4 tablespoon water

½ cup unsweetened cocoa

3 eggs

1 cup buttermilk

2 teaspoons vanilla extract

2 tablespoons red food coloring

2½ cups all-purpose flour

½ cup cornstarch

1½ teaspoons baking powder

1½ cups sugar

For the frosting

1 cup (8 ounces) cream cheese

3 tablespoons unsalted butter

3 tablespoons sugar

1 teaspoon vanilla extract

Preheat oven to 375°F. Grease two 9-inch layer cake pans and line the bottoms with parchment paper.

Place the butter, water, and cocoa in a small saucepan and heat gently, without boiling, stirring until the butter is melted and the mixture is smooth. Remove from the heat and let cool slightly.

Beat together the eggs, buttermilk, vanilla extract, and food coloring until frothy. Beat in the butter mixture. Sift together the flour, cornstarch, and baking powder, then stir quickly and evenly into the mixture with the sugar.

Divide the batter between the prepared pans and bake for 25 to 30 minutes, or until risen and firm to the touch. Cool in the pans for 3 to 4 minutes, then turn out and finish cooling on a wire rack.

For the frosting: Beat together all the ingredients until smooth. Use about half of the frosting to sandwich the cakes together, then spread the remainder over the top, swirling with a metal spatula.

pound cake with orange glaze

Perfect with a cup of tea or coffee, this simple pound cake
is also great sitting under some fresh fruit.

serves 6

2 cups all-purpose flour

1 teaspoon baking powder

¼ teaspoon baking soda

½ teaspoon salt

1 cup (2 sticks) unsalted butter

1¼ cups sugar

1 tablespoon grated lemon zest

1 tablespoon grated orange zest

4 eggs

½ cup buttermilk

1 teaspoon vanilla extract

For the glaze

1 cup confectioners' sugar

1½ tablespoons fresh orange juice, or as needed

1 tablespoon freshly grated orange zest

Preheat oven to 325°F. Butter one loaf pan, and dust with flour. Set aside.

Sift together the flour, baking powder, baking soda, and salt in a mixing bowl. Set aside.

In a large mixing bowl, use an electric mixer to cream the butter, sugar, and zests until very light and creamy. Beat in the eggs, one at time, beating very thoroughly after each addition. Use a spatula to mix in flour alternately with the buttermilk, ending with flour. Add the vanilla extract. Scrape the batter into the prepared loaf pan.

Bake for 1 hour to 1 hour 15 minutes, or until a tester inserted in the center comes out clean. Remove and let rest for 15 minutes, then turn onto a cooling rack. Let cool 15 more minutes before glazing.

To make the glaze: Stir together the glaze ingredients, adding enough orange juice to get a smooth spreadable consistency. Apply to the top of the warm cake. Let the pound cake cool completely before slicing.

carrot cake with cream cheese frosting

If someone created a list of the greatest cake/frosting combinations of all time, this dense, moist carrot cake topped with cream cheese frosting has to be at the top.

serves 8

2 cups all-purpose flour

1 teaspoon salt

2 teaspoons baking powder

1 teaspoon baking soda

2 teaspoons cinnamon

½ teaspoon ground ginger

2 cups sugar

1¼ cups vegetable oil

4 large eggs

¼ cup (½ stick) melted butter

2 cups raw grated carrots

1 (8 ounce) can crushed pineapple, drained

½ cup chopped pecans

½ cup chopped walnuts

For the frosting

½ cup (1 stick) unsalted butter, softened

1 cup (8 ounces) cream cheese, softened

1 tablespoon milk

1 teaspoon vanilla

1 pound confectioners' sugar

Preheat oven to 350°F. Whisk together the flour, salt, baking powder, baking soda, cinnamon, and ginger in a mixing bowl for a minute or two; reserve until needed.

In another mixing bowl, combine the sugar, oil, and eggs. Whisk until thoroughly combined. Whisk in the melted butter. Use a spatula to stir in the carrots, pineapple, and nuts. Stir in the flour mixture in two additions.

Scrape the batter into a lightly greased 13x9-inch cake pan. Bake for about 40 minutes, or until the top springs back slightly when gently touched with your finger. Remove and allow to cool completely before frosting.

To make the frosting: Using an electric mixer, beat together the butter, cream cheese, milk, and vanilla extract until light and fluffy. Gradually beat in the confectioners' sugar to form a smooth frosting. Spread evenly over the cooled cake.

boston cream pie

Sure you can make this cake from scratch, but let's face it, in this classic American dessert the cake is nothing more than a chocolate and pastry cream delivery system.

serves 6-8

1 (18.25 ounce) package white or yellow cake mix, prepared according to directions and cooled

For the pastry cream
7 tablespoons sugar
2 tablespoons cornstarch
3 large eggs
1 cup whipping cream
1 cup whole milk
1 tablespoon butter
1½ teaspoons vanilla extract
Pinch of salt

For the chocolate topping (called a ganache)
4 ounces high-quality bittersweet chocolate, chopped
½ cup heavy cream
1 teaspoon butter

For the pastry cream: Combine the sugar, cornstarch, and eggs in a mixing bowl; whisk vigorously until the mixture is light and creamy; set aside.

Bring the cream, milk, and butter to a boil in a small saucepan over medium-high heat. Quickly whisk in the egg mixture, and boil, stirring constantly, for exactly one minute. The mixture should become very thick, very quickly. Remove from heat and strain into a bowl. Cover the surface with plastic wrap, and let cool at room temperature for 20 minutes, then refrigerate until completely cold; overnight is best. Before completing the cake, whisk in the vanilla extract, and a pinch of salt.

When your pastry cream is ready, and your cakes have been baked and completely cooled, you're ready to assemble. Place one layer down on a cake plate, top with the pastry cream and lay the other cake gently on top. If you want less cake you can just use one layer, sliced through the center to make two thinner layers.

For the chocolate topping: Place the chocolate in a heat-proof bowl and set aside. Bring the cream and butter to a simmer over medium-high heat, then quickly pour over the chocolate. Let sit for 3 minutes, then gently whisk to combine. When the mixture has thickened slightly, yet is still thin enough to pour, spread evenly over the top of the cake. Refrigerate until the chocolate has firmed up completely before slicing and serving.

cinnamon swirl sour cream bundt cake

The word "coffee" is not part of the title of this recipe, but make no mistake, this is a coffee cake. In fact, if you don't drink coffee, please start before attempting this moist, spicy cake.

serves 6-8

2½ cups all-purpose flour

1 teaspoon baking powder

1 teaspoon baking soda

½ teaspoon salt

¾ cup (1½ sticks) unsalted butter

1½ cups sugar

3 large eggs

1 cup sour cream

1 teaspoon vanilla extract

½ cup chopped walnuts, optional

For the swirl

1 tablespoon ground cinnamon

3 tablespoons firmly packed light brown sugar

2 tablespoons sugar

For the glaze

1 cup confectioners' sugar

1½ tablespoons milk

1 teaspoon ground cinnamon, or to taste

Preheat oven to 350°F. Whisk together the flour, baking powder, baking soda, and salt in a mixing bowl for a minute; reserve until needed.

Cream the butter and sugar together until light and fluffy. Beat in the eggs one at a time, mixing thoroughly before adding the next. Beat in the sour cream and vanilla extract until combined. Add the flour mixture, stirring just until combined. Stir in the walnuts.

Butter a 10-inch Bundt pan, and lightly dust with flour. Pour half the batter into the pan and spread evenly. Mix the ingredients for the swirl in a small bowl. Sprinkle evenly around the center of the batter. Cover with the rest of the batter.

Bake for 50 minutes, or until a tester inserted in the center comes out clean. Let cool 20 minutes before removing from the pan.

For the glaze: Add the confectioners' sugar to a small mixing bowl, stir in enough milk to create a thick, but pourable glaze. Stir in the cinnamon to taste. Drizzle over the top of the cake. Once the icing is set, slice and serve with lots of hot coffee.

lemon poppy seed muffins

Imagine a day you are so busy you miss breakfast, and have to settle for grabbing a lemon poppy seed muffin on the way out. That is a pretty good morning!

makes 12 muffins

2 cups all-purpose flour

½ teaspoon salt

1½ teaspoons baking powder

¼ teaspoon baking soda

½ cup (1 stick) unsalted butter, softened

1 cup sugar

Finely grated zest from 2 lemons

2 large eggs

2 tablespoons lemon juice

1 cup sour cream

2 tablespoons poppy seeds

For the glaze

1 tablespoon lemon juice

3 tablespoons confectioners' sugar

Preheat oven to 350°F. Whisk together the flour, salt, baking powder, and baking soda in a bowl, and reserve until needed.

In a mixing bowl, beat the butter, sugar, and lemon zest, until light and creamy. Beat in the eggs one at a time, mixing thoroughly before adding the next. Stir in a third of the flour mixture until just combined. Stir in the lemon juice, and half of the sour cream until combined.

Add half of the remaining flour mixture, and stir until combined. Stir in the remaining sour cream. Stir in the rest of the flour mixture, and then the poppy seeds.

Line a 12-cup muffin tin with paper baking cups. Fill each to the top with batter. Bake about 30 minutes, or until golden brown and a tester inserted in the center comes out clean. While the muffins are baking, mix the lemon juice and confectioners' sugar together to form a thin glaze.

Remove the muffins from the oven when ready, and allow to cool for 5 minutes. Brush the lemon glaze evenly over the top of each muffin. This is not intended to be a frosting, but just a very light glaze to give the tops a little shine and extra kiss of lemon flavor.

When cool enough to handle, remove muffins from the tins and cool completely on a rack before serving.

blueberry muffins

The sour cream gives these blueberry muffins a nice richness, and keeps them moist and tender.

makes 16 muffins

3 cups all-purpose flour

¾ teaspoon salt

1 tablespoon baking powder

½ teaspoon baking soda

1 cup sugar

½ cup (1 stick) butter, softened

Finely grated zest from one lemon

2 tablespoons vegetable oil

2 large eggs

1 cup sour cream

½ cup milk

½ teaspoon lemon extract, optional

2 cups fresh blueberries

Preheat oven to 375°F. Sift together the flour, salt, baking powder, and baking soda into a bowl; reserve.

In a large mixing bowl, beat the sugar, butter, lemon zest, and vegetable oil until light and creamy. Beat in the eggs one at a time. Whisk in the sour cream, milk, and lemon extract.

Add half the dry ingredients, and stir until just barely combined. Add the remaining dry ingredients, along with the blueberries, and fold with a spatula until just combined.

Line the muffin tins with paper baking cups. Fill each to the top with batter. Bake for 30 minutes to a beautiful golden brown. When cool enough to handle, remove muffins from the tins and serve.

whoopie pies

You have to love any recipe whose name comes from such a joyous exclamation! "Whoopie!" indeed.

makes 8-10

2 cups all-purpose flour

3 tablespoons unsweetened cocoa powder

½ teaspoon baking soda

¼ teaspoon salt

½ cup (1 stick) unsalted butter, softened

1 cup packed brown sugar

1 large egg

1¼ teaspoons vanilla extract

½ cup buttermilk

For the filling

½ cup (4 ounces) softened cream cheese

1 (7 ounce) jar marshmallow crème

Preheat oven to 375°F. Add the flour, cocoa powder, baking soda, and salt to a mixing bowl. Stir the mixture enthusiastically with a whisk to combine and aerate. Reserve until needed.

Cream the butter and brown sugar in a large mixing bowl with an electric mixer until light and fluffy. Beat in the egg and vanilla until thoroughly combined. Add a third of the flour mixture; stir until combined. Add half the buttermilk; stir until combined. Add half the remaining flour; stir until combined. Add the remaining buttermilk, stir in, and finally mix in the last of the flour.

Line two heavy-duty baking sheets with silicon baking mats or parchment paper. Spoon the batter on the baking sheets, forming rounds about ½-inch high and 3 inches wide. As long as the batter is spooned on about ½ inch thick, you can make these as small or large as you like. The most important thing is they all remain the same size, so they bake evenly.

Bake for 12 to 14 minutes, or until the tops look cooked, and are slightly firm to the touch (be gentle). Remove and let rest for 15 minutes on the baking sheets. Remove to racks and let cool completely before filling.

To make the filling: In a mixing bowl beat the cream cheese until light and fluffy. Fold in the marshmallow crème. Spread a couple spoonfuls of filling on the flat side of one of the cakes, and top with another to form a sandwich.

double chocolate muffins

Chocolate/chocolate muffins—perfect for breakfast, a snack, or even dessert! Perfection!

makes 8 muffins

¾ **cup self-rising flour**

½ **cup cocoa powder**

½ **cup (1 stick) butter, softened**

½ **cup sugar**

2 **large eggs**

½ **cup semisweet chocolate chips**

Preheat the oven to 375°F. Line a 12-cup muffin tin with 8 paper baking liners.

In a bowl, sift together the flour and cocoa powder.

In a large mixing bowl, beat together the butter, sugar, and eggs until smooth.

Add half the dry ingredients and stir until combined; add the remaining dry ingredients. Fold in the chocolate chips until combined.

Spoon the batter into the prepared muffin cups.

Bake in the preheated oven for 20 to 25 minutes, or until well risen and springy to the touch. Transfer to a wire rack to cool completely.

pumpkin crumb cake

Here is a delicious cake featuring the surprising presence of pumpkin. Perfect for an autumn brunch.

serves 6

1¾ cups all-purpose flour

1½ teaspoons pumpkin pie spice

1 teaspoon baking soda

1 teaspoon baking powder

¾ teaspoon salt

½ cup (1 stick) butter, room temperature

1¾ cups sugar

3 large eggs

1 cup canned pure pumpkin

1 teaspoon vanilla extract

½ cup milk

¾ cup chopped walnuts, optional

For the topping

²/₃ cup plus 2 tablespoons rolled oats

½ cup all-purpose flour

½ cup light brown sugar

½ teaspoon cinnamon

6 tablespoons unsalted butter

Preheat oven to 350°F. Grease a 9x5x3-inch loaf pan and line with parchment paper.

For the topping: Combine ²/₃ cup oats, flour, brown sugar, and cinnamon in processor. Add the butter and cut in until crumbly. Transfer mixture to medium bowl. Stir in the remaining 2 tablespoons oats. Set aside.

Sift the flour, pumpkin spice, baking soda, baking powder, and salt into a bowl.

In a separate bowl, with an electric mixer beat the butter until smooth. Gradually beat in the sugar and 1 egg at a time. Add the pumpkin and vanilla extract to the wet batter mix.

Gradually beat the dry ingredients into the batter. Slowly add the milk, and stir in the walnuts, optional. Transfer the batter to the prepared pan and spread with the topping mix.

Bake the loaf cake until a tester inserted into center comes out clean, about 55 minutes. Cool in the pan for 15 minutes. Turn the cake out onto a rack and cool completely.

pies

apple pie

This recipe is dedicated to everyone who realizes that, "As American as apple pie", is much more than just a saying.

serves 6

For the crust

2½ cups all-purpose flour

1 cup (2 sticks) ice cold butter, cut into ½ inch pieces

½ teaspoon salt

7 tablespoons ice water

1 tablespoon cider vinegar

For the filling

6 baking apples, peeled, cored, and thinly sliced

½ lemon, juiced

1 cup sugar

3 tablespoons cornstarch

Pinch of nutmeg

½ teaspoon cinnamon

2 tablespoons butter

1 beaten egg to glaze the crust

Preheat oven to 375°F.

For the crust: Add the flour into the bowl of a food processor, with the regular blade attached. Add the butter and salt. Pulse until the mixture resembles coarse crumbs. Mix the water and vinegar together. Pour half into the processor, and pulse. Add the rest of the mixture, and again pulse until the dough starts to clump together. Do not over-mix. Transfer the dough onto a work surface, and shape the dough into a ball with your hands. Cut in half and shape each half into a disk about 5-inches wide. Wrap in plastic and chill in the refrigerator for 30 minutes.

For the filling: Toss the apple slices with the lemon juice in a large mixing bowl. Add the rest of the filling ingredients, except the butter, and mix until well combined.

Roll half the dough out on a lightly floured surface to form the bottom crust, for a 9-inch pie with a few inches to spare all around. Place and press into the pan. Pour the apple mixture into the bottom crust. Dot the apples with the butter. Roll out the second half of the dough and cover the mounded apples. Pinch the edges so that both crusts are sealed all the way around the pan. Go around the edge with a fork to make a design, or "crimp" the edge using your fingers. Cut a few slashes in the top crust and brush with the beaten egg. Bake for 1 to 1½ hours, until the crust is nicely browned, and the apples are tender when tested through the slits on the top. If the crust begins to brown too quickly, tent with foil. Let cool before serving.

sweet potato pie

And you thought sweet potatoes were just something you picked at once a year around the Thanksgiving table.

serves 8-10

For the crust

1¼ cups all-purpose flour, plus extra for dusting

½ teaspoon salt

¼ teaspoon sugar

1½ tablespoons butter, diced

3 tablespoons vegetable shortening, diced

2 to 2½ tablespoons ice-cold water

For the filling

2 cups cooked mashed sweet potatoes

3 extra-large eggs, beaten

½ cup firmly packed dark brown sugar

1½ cups evaporated milk

3 tablespoons butter, melted

2 teaspoons vanilla extract

1 teaspoon ground cinnamon

1 teaspoon ground nutmeg

½ teaspoon salt

Freshly whipped cream, to serve

Preheat oven to 425°F.

To make the pie crsut: Sift the flour, salt, and sugar into a bowl. Add the butter and vegetable shortening to the bowl and rub in with the fingertips until fine crumbs form. Sprinkle over 2 tablespoons of the water and mix with a fork until a soft dough forms. Add ½ tablespoon of water if the dough is too dry. Wrap in plastic wrap and chill for at least 1 hour.

For the filling: Put the sweet potatoes into a bowl and beat in the eggs and sugar until very smooth. Beat in the remaining ingredients, except the whipped cream, then set aside.

Roll out the dough on a lightly floured surface into a thin 11-inch circle and use to line a 9-inch pie pan, about 1½-inches high. Trim off the excess dough and press the floured tines of a fork around the edge.

Prick the base of the pastry shell all over with the fork and place crumpled kitchen foil in the center. Bake in the oven for 12 minutes, or until lightly golden.

Remove the pastry shell from the oven, take out the foil, pour the filling into the shell, and return to the oven for an additional 10 minutes. Reduce the oven temperature to 325°F and bake for a further 35 minutes, or until a tester inserted into the center comes out clean. Let cool on a cooling rack. Serve warm or at room temperature with whipped cream.

lemon meringue pie

This classic pie has been a great favorite for decades. It has three distinct parts: the crisp pastry base; the tangy, smooth lemon center; and the crispy meringue topping.

serves 8-10

9 ounces ready-made unsweetened pie dough, thawed if frozen

For the filling

All-purpose flour, for dusting

3 tablespoons cornstarch

½ cup sugar

Grated rind of 3 lemons

1¼ cups cold water

⅔ cup lemon juice

3 egg yolks

½ stick unsalted butter, diced

For the meringue

3 egg whites

1 cup sugar

1 teaspoon sugar

Preheat oven to 400°F. Grease a 10-inch fluted tart pan. Roll out the pastry on a lightly floured surface into a circle 2 inches larger than the tart pan. Press pastry into the pan, and trim the edge. Prick the base with a fork and chill, uncovered, in the refrigerator for 30 minutes.

Line the pastry shell with parchment paper and fill with pie weights. Bake on a baking sheet for 15 minutes. Remove the weights and paper and return to the oven for 10 minutes, or until the pastry is dry and just colored. Remove from the oven and reduce the temperature to 300°F.

For the filling: Put the cornstarch, sugar, and lemon rind in a pan. Pour in a little water and blend to a smooth paste. Add the remaining water and the lemon juice. Bring the mixture to a boil, stirring constantly. Simmer for 1 minute, or until smooth and glossy. Remove from the heat and beat in the egg yolks, one at a time, then beat in the butter. Put the pan in a bowl of cold water to cool the filling. Spoon into the pastry shell.

For the meringue: Whisk the egg whites with an electric mixer until soft peaks form. Add the sugar gradually, mixing well with each addition, until the whites are glossy and firm. Spoon over the filling and swirl into peaks. Bake for 20 to 30 minutes, or until the meringue is crispy but still soft in the center.

pecan pie

The classic nut pie is the ideal change of pace from soft, fruit-filled varieties.

serves 8

For the crust

1¾ cups all-purpose flour, plus extra for dusting

½ cup butter

2 tablespoons sugar

For the filling

5 tablespoons butter

½ cup firmly packed light brown sugar

²/₃ cup dark corn syrup

2 extra-large eggs, beaten

1 teaspoon vanilla extract

1 cup pecans

Preheat oven to 400°F.

For the crust: Place the flour in a bowl and rub in the butter using your fingertips until it resembles fine breadcrumbs. Stir in the sugar and add enough cold water to mix to a firm dough. Wrap in plastic wrap and chill for 15 minutes, until firm enough to roll out.

Roll out the dough on a lightly floured surface and use to line a 9-inch round, spring form tart pan. Prick the bottom with a fork. Chill for 15 minutes.

Place the tart pan on a baking sheet, line with a sheet of parchment paper, and fill with pie weights. Bake for 10 minutes. Remove the paper and pie weights and bake for an additional 5 minutes. Reduce the oven temperature to 350°F.

For the filling: Place the butter, brown sugar, and corn syrup in a saucepan and heat gently until melted. Remove from the heat and quickly beat in the eggs and vanilla extract. Coarsely chop the pecans and stir into the mixture.

Pour into the tart shell and bake for 35 to 40 minutes, until the filling is just set. Serve warm or cold.

blueberry pie

With fresh blueberries, you can go "easy" with the sugar.
Their natural sweetness is just about perfect.

serves 8

For the crust

2 cups all-purpose flour
1 cup shortening
½ teaspoon salt
¼ cup milk
2 tablespoon vinegar

For the filling

¾ cup sugar
3 tablespoon cornstarch
¼ teaspoon salt
½ teaspoon ground cinnamon
½ teaspoon ground nutmeg
4 cups fresh blueberries
1 tablespoon butter

Preheat oven to 425°F.

For the crust: Sift the flour and salt into a bowl and cut in the shortening with a pastry blender or your fingertips until it is the size of small peas. Using a fork to lightly mix the ingredients, add the vinegar and milk just enough to moisten the dry ingredients, being sure to add the milk 1 tablespoon at a time. The dough will be sticky.

Divide the dough in half, form it into 2 equal-size balls, then flatten each ball into a disk. On a lightly floured surface, roll out one portion of dough to a thickness of about ⅛ inch, fit it into a 9-inch pie pan.

For the filling: Mix sugar, cornstarch, salt, cinnamon, and nutmeg, and sprinkle over blueberries.

Pour the berry mixture into the crust, and dot with butter. Cut remaining dough into ½-inch-wide strips, and make lattice top. Crimp and flute the edges.

Bake the pie on the lower shelf of the oven for about 50 minutes, or until the crust is golden brown.

cherry pie

Apple pie may be the traditional American dish, but cherry pie may be a better choice—especially since cherries reach their peak over the fourth of July!

serves 8

For the crust

1 cup all-purpose flour, plus extra for dusting

¼ teaspoon baking powder

½ teaspoon allspice

½ teaspoon salt

¼ cup sugar

4 tablespoons (½ stick) cold unsalted butter, diced, plus extra for greasing

1 egg, beaten, plus extra for glazing

For the filling

2 pounds pitted fresh cherries or drained canned cherries

½ cup sugar

½ teaspoon almond extract

2 teaspoon cherry brandy

¼ teaspoon allspice

2 tablespoon cornstarch

2 tablespoon water

2 tablespoon unsalted butter, diced

Preheat the oven to 425°F.

For the crust: Sift the flour and baking powder into a large bowl. Stir in the allspice, salt, and sugar. Rub in the butter with your fingertips until the mixture resembles fine breadcrumbs. Add the beaten egg and mix to a firm dough. Cut the dough in half and roll each half into a ball. Wrap in plastic wrap and chill in the refrigerator for 30 minutes.

Grease a 9-inch round tart pan. Roll out the pie dough into two 12-inch rounds. Use one to line the tart pan, trimming the edge to leave an overhang of ½ inch.

For the filling: Put half of the cherries and the sugar in a large saucepan. Bring to a simmer over low heat, stirring, for 5 minutes, or until the sugar has dissolved. Stir in the almond extract, brandy, and allspice. In a separate bowl, mix the cornstarch and water to form a paste. Remove the saucepan from the heat, stir in the cornstarch paste, then return to the heat and stir continuously until the mixture boils and thickens. Let cool a little. Stir in the remaining cherries, pour into the pastry shell, then dot with the butter.

Cut the remaining dough round into long strips about ½-inch wide and form a lattice. Trim the ends and seal and crimp the edges. Bake the pie on the lower shelf of the oven for about 50 minutes, or until the crust is golden brown. Serve warm or at room temperature.

mississippi mud pie

A chocolaty crust topped with a gooey chocolate filling and decorated with chocolate sprinkles and curls! The only thing more decadent is to serve it with ice cream!

serves 8

For the crust
1½ cups all-purpose flour, plus extra for dusting

2 tablespoon unsweetened cocoa

½ cup (1 stick) unsalted butter

2 tablespoon sugar

1–2 tablespoon cold water

For the filling
¾ cup (1½ sticks) unsalted butter

1¾ cups firmly packed dark brown sugar

4 eggs, lightly beaten

4 tablespoon unsweetened cocoa, sifted

5½ ounces semisweet chocolate

1¼ cups light cream

1 teaspoon chocolate extract

To decorate
2 cups heavy cream, whipped

Chocolate flakes and curls

Preheat the oven to 375°F.

For the crust: Sift the flour and cocoa into a mixing bowl. Rub in the butter with your fingertips until the mixture resembles fine breadcrumbs. Stir in the sugar and enough cold water to mix to a soft dough. Wrap the dough in plastic wrap and let chill in the refrigerator for 15 minutes.

Roll out the dough on a lightly floured surface and use to line a 9-inch spring-form tart pan. Line with parchment paper and fill with dried beans. Bake in the preheated oven for 15 minutes. Remove from the oven and take out the paper and beans. Bake the pastry shell for an additional 10 minutes.

For the filling: Beat the butter and sugar together in a bowl and gradually beat in the eggs with the cocoa. Melt the chocolate in a heatproof bowl set over a saucepan of gently simmering water, then beat it into the mixture with the light cream and the chocolate extract.

Reduce the oven temperature to 325°F. Pour the mixture into the pastry shell and bake for 45 minutes, or until the filling has set gently.

Let the mud pie cool completely, then transfer it to a serving plate. Cover with the whipped cream and decorate with chocolate flakes and curls. Chill until ready to serve.

desserts

vanilla ice cream with chocolate sauce

Simply put—there is nothing like homemade ice cream—
except the addition of warm chocolate sauce.

*makes 1 quart ice cream
and 1¼ cups sauce*

For the ice cream
4 large egg yolks
1 cup sugar
1 cup whole milk
2 cups whipping cream
1 whole vanilla bean

For the sauce
½ cup heavy cream
**²/₃ cup (4 ounces)
semisweet chocolate,
broken into small pieces**
**2 tablespoons orange
liqueur**

For the ice cream: Add egg yolks, sugar, milk, and cream to a heavy-bottomed saucepan. Whisk thoroughly to combine.

Split the vanilla bean lengthwise and scrape out the seeds with the back of the knife. Add the pod and the seeds to the mixture. Place over medium-low heat.

Cook, stirring constantly with a silicon spatula, until the mixture reaches a temperature of 175°F. This will be just below a simmer, but best to use a thermometer. Do not allow the mixture to boil.

Remove from heat and place saucepan over a bowl of ice water to cool, stirring occasionally. Remove the vanilla bean and pour the cooled mixture into a container with a tight-fitting lid. Cover and refrigerate mixture at least 4 hours, or overnight for best results.

Freeze mixture in an ice cream maker according to the manufacturer's instructions. Transfer the mixture back into the container, cover and allow to harden in the freezer for a couple hours before serving.

For the sauce: Bring the cream gently to a boil in a small heavy-bottomed pan over low heat. Remove the pan from the heat, add the broken chocolate, and stir until smooth.

Stir in the liqueur and serve immediately, or keep the sauce warm until required.

lemon curd

Lemon curd is delicious and easy to make. It is best eaten fresh but can be stored for up to 2 months in a refrigerator. Use on scones, to make lemon tarts, or as a filling for sponge cakes.

makes about 3 cups

3 large lemons, washed in hot water
1½ cups sugar
3 eggs, beaten
¾ cup (1½ sticks) butter

Prepare two or three 8-ounce canning jars. To sterilize the jars, wash them in soapy water and rinse well, and then heat them in a moderate oven for 5 minutes.

Carefully grate the rind from each of the lemons using a fine grater. Make sure you only take the yellow rind and not the bitter white pith.

Cut the lemons in half and squeeze out all the juice, then sieve to remove the seeds.

Place a medium-sized heatproof bowl over a saucepan of simmering water and add the lemon rind, juice and sugar. Mix together well until the sugar has dissolved.

Add the eggs and the butter cut into small pieces and continue to stir for 25 to 30 minutes until the butter has melted and the mixture begins to thicken. Beat well, then turn into the sterilized jars. Cover and label before storing. Once opened the lemon curd will keep for up to 2 months in the refrigerator.

very berry crisp

This super-easy fruit dessert can be made with any combination of berries. Just don't forget to put vanilla ice cream on the grocery list (or better yet, make some homemade).

serves 6-8

2 pounds mixed berries – raspberries, blackberries, strawberries, blueberries – fresh or frozen, thawed

¾ cup sugar

1 teaspoon fresh lemon juice

1 tablespoon cornstarch

⅛ teaspoon cinnamon

For the topping

½ cup flour

½ cup firmly packed light brown sugar

⅔ cup quick-cooking rolled oats

¼ teaspoon ground ginger

⅛ teaspoon salt

4 tablespoons cold butter, cut in small pieces

Preheat oven to 375°F. In a bowl, combine the berries, sugar, lemon juice, cornstarch, and cinnamon; mix to combine thoroughly. Pour into a lightly-buttered 2-quart baking dish.

For the topping: In the same bowl, combine the flour, brown sugar, oats, ginger, salt, and butter. Using a pastry cutter or your fingertips, cut or rub the butter into the dry ingredients to form a very coarse, crumbly mixture.

Spread the topping over the berries and bake for 40 minutes, or until a bubbly, well-browned crust forms.

Let sit for at least 15 minutes, before serving warm with ice cream.

new york cheesecake with fruit sauce

Apples are okay, but this decadent dessert begs the question,
why isn't New York called "The Big Cheesecake"?

serves 8-10

½ cup butter

1¾ cups finely crushed
grahams crackers

1 tablespoon sugar

2 pounds cream cheese

1¼ cups sugar

2 tablespoons all-purpose
flour

1 teaspoon vanilla extract

Finely grated zest
of 1 orange

Finely grated zest
of 1 lemon

3 eggs

2 egg yolks

1¼ cups heavy cream

For the sauce

1½ cups (8 ounces)
berries, such as
blackberries or raspberries

2 tablespoons water

2 to 3 tablespoons sugar

2 tablespoons fruit liqueur,
such as crème de cassis
or crème de framboise

Preheat the oven to 350°F. Place a small saucepan over low heat, melt the butter and remove from heat. Stir in crushed crackers and 1 tablespoon sugar. Mix. Press the cracker mixture into the bottom of a 9-inch cake pan. Bake for 10 minutes. Remove and cool.

Increase oven temperature to 400°F.

With an electric mixer, beat the cream cheese until creamy and gradually add the sugar and flour and beat until smooth. Beat in the vanilla extract, orange and lemon zest, then one at a time, beat in the eggs and egg yolks. Finally beat in the heavy cream. The mixture should be light and whippy.

Grease the sides of the cake pan and pour in the filling. Transfer to the preheated oven and bake for 15 minutes. Reduce heat to 200°F and bake for an additional 30 minutes. Turn the oven off and leave to cool for 2 hours. Cover and refrigerate overnight.

For the sauce: Put all the ingredients into a small, heavy-bottomed pan and heat gently until the sugar has dissolved and the fruit juices run. Process to a paste in a food processor, then push through a non-metallic strainer into a serving bowl to remove the seeds. Add more sugar, if necessary, and serve warm or cold.

bread and butter pudding with whiskey sauce

Is there any better fate for a loaf of stale bread than to be turned into this amazing Southern treat? This is the ultimate comfort food dessert, and perfect for a large group.

serves 10

For the bread pudding

6 large eggs

1½ cups sugar

4 cups milk

1 cup heavy cream

1 tablespoon bourbon whiskey

1 tablespoon vanilla extract

1 teaspoon ground cinnamon

Pinch of allspice

1 (1 pound) loaf day-old French bread, torn into 1-inch chunks

4 tablespoons (½ stick) butter, melted

½ cup golden raisins

For the whiskey sauce

1 cups sugar

½ cup (1 stick) butter

½ cup corn syrup

¼ cup bourbon whiskey, or to taste

Preheat oven to 325°F. In a mixing bowl, whisk together the eggs and sugar until light and creamy. Add the milk, cream, whiskey, vanilla, cinnamon, and allspice. Whisk thoroughly until combined.

Scatter the bread in a 9 x 13-inch baking dish, and drizzle over the melted butter. Toss until coated. Top with the raisins. Cover with the custard mixture. Let rest for 30 minutes to allow the bread to soak up the custard.

Bake about 40 minutes, or until the custard is set and the top is browned. Let cool for 15 minutes before serving. May be served warm, room temperature, or cold.

To make the sauce: Mix the sugar, butter, and corn syrup in saucepan over low heat. Stir until the butter is melted, the sugar is dissolved, and the mixture is heated through. Whisk in the whiskey. May be served warm, or at room temperature.

rhubarb crumble

Rhubarb's unique, tart flavor makes it a great complement for this easy dessert's sweet crumble topping.

serves 6

2 pounds rhubarb (about 6 cups cut rhubarb)

½ cup sugar

Grated zest and juice of 1 orange

2½ cups plain or wholewheat flour

4 tablespoons butter

⅔ cup firmly packed light brown sugar

1 teaspoon ground ginger

Preheat oven to 375°F. Cut the rhubarb into 1-inch lengths and place in a 3-pint flameproof dish with the sugar and the orange zest and juice.

To make the crumble: Place the flour in a mixing bowl and rub in the butter with your fingertips until the mixture resembles bread crumbs. Stir in the brown sugar and the ginger.

Spread the crumble evenly over the fruit and press down lightly using a fork.

Bake in the center of the oven on a baking sheet for 25 to 30 minutes until the crumble is golden brown

Serve warm with heavy cream, ice cream, or yogurt.

peach cobbler

Whenever people do those word association exercises, and the word is "summer", one of the most common responses is, "peach cobbler".

serves 4-6

For the filling

6 peaches, peeled and sliced

4 tablespoons sugar

½ tablespoon lemon juice

1½ teaspoon cornstarch

½ teaspoon almond or vanilla extract

Vanilla or butter pecan ice cream

For the topping

1½ cups all-purpose flour

½ cup sugar

1½ teaspoons baking powder

½ teaspoon salt

6 tablespoons diced butter

1 egg

6 tablespoons milk

Preheat oven to 425°F.

Place the peaches in a 9-inch square ovenproof dish. Add the sugar, lemon juice, cornstarch and almond extract and toss together. Bake for 20 minutes.

To make the topping: Sift the flour, all but 2 tablespoons of the sugar, the baking powder, and the salt into a bowl. Rub in the butter with your fingertips until the mixture resembles breadcrumbs. Mix the egg and 5 tablespoons of the milk in a jug, then mix into the dry ingredients with a fork until a soft, sticky dough forms. If the dough seems too dry, stir in the extra tablespoon of milk.

Reduce the oven temperature to 400°F. Remove the peaches from the oven and drop spoonfuls of the topping over the surface, without smoothing. Sprinkle with the remaining sugar, return to the oven and bake for a further 15 minutes or until the topping is golden brown and firm— the topping will spread as it cooks. Serve hot or at room temperature with ice cream.

breakfast treats

blueberry pancakes

When it's summer in Maine, the state's blueberries feature at every meal, starting with breakfast, when they flavor muffins and pancakes. For a complete New England breakfast, serve these with Vermont maple syrup.

makes 10-12 pancakes

1 cup all-purpose flour

2 tablespoons sugar

2 teaspoons baking powder

½ teaspoon salt

1 cup buttermilk

3 tablespoons butter, melted

1 large egg

1 cup (5 ounces) blueberries, rinsed and patted dry

To serve

Butter

Warm maple syrup

Preheat oven to 275°F. Sift the flour, sugar, baking powder, and salt together into a large bowl and make a well in the center.

Beat the buttermilk, butter, and egg together in a separate small bowl, then pour the mixture into the well in the dry ingredients. Beat the dry ingredients into the liquid, gradually drawing them in from the side, until a smooth batter forms. Gently stir in the blueberries.

Heat a large skillet over medium-high heat until a splash of water dances on the surface. Use a pastry brush or crumpled piece of paper towel and the oil to lightly grease the base of the skillet.

Use a ladle to drop about 4 tablespoons of batter into the skillet and spread it out into a 4-inch round. Continue adding as many pancakes as will fit in your skillet. Leave the pancakes to cook until small bubbles appear on the surface, then flip them over and cook for a further 1 to 2 minutes until the bottoms are golden brown.

Transfer the pancakes to a warmed plate and keep warm in the oven while you cook the remaining pancakes, lightly greasing the skillet before each batch. Serve with a pat of butter on top of each pancake and warm maple syrup for pouring over.

new orleans-style french toast

This recipe was born as a deliciously decadent solution for what to do with stale loaves!

serves 4-6

5 large eggs

1 cup milk

½ cup cream

Pinch of salt

1 tablespoon sugar

2 teaspoons vanilla extract

½ teaspoon cinnamon

¹/₈ teaspoon allspice

12 thick slices day-old French bread (use a regular sized loaf, not the skinny baguette type)

6 tablespoons butter, plus more as needed

Preheat oven to 375°F. In a large mixing bowl, whisk together the eggs, milk, cream, salt, sugar, vanilla extract, cinnamon, and allspice. Soak the bread slices in the custard mixture for at least 20 minutes, or until completely saturated.

In a large nonstick skillet, lightly brown the slices in batches, in a few tablespoons of butter over medium heat; about 2 minutes per side. Don't cook too dark, as additional browning will occur in the oven.

Transfer to lightly buttered, foil-lined sheet pans, and bake for 10 minutes. After 10 minutes, remove, and turn each slice over. Put back in the oven for another 10 to 15 minutes, or until browned and the bread springs back slightly when tested with a finger.

Serve immediately.

cheese blintzes with strawberry sauce

Blintzes are a wonderful special-occasion breakfast or brunch treat. Eastern European immigrants brought these wonderful cheese-filled crêpes to America, and we're all better for it.

makes 8-10

For the batter

1 cup whole milk

¼ cup cold water

2 large eggs

1 cup all-purpose flour

¹/₈ teaspoon salt

1 tablespoon sugar

3 tablespoons
vegetable oil

Vegetable oil spray for
cooking the crêpes

For the filling

1½ cups ricotta cheese

½ cup (4 ounces)
cream cheese

3 tablespoons
confectioners' sugar

1 teaspoon freshly grated
lemon zest

1 large egg

For the sauce

¾ cup strawberry
preserves, or any other
fruit jam or jelly

¼ cup water

Preheat oven to 400°F.

For the batter: Pour the milk, water, eggs, flour, salt, sugar, and vegetable oil in a blender; blend until very smooth. Refrigerate for 2 hours.

For the filling: Combine the ricotta cheese, cream cheese, confectioners' sugar, lemon zest, and egg in a blender and blend until smooth. Refrigerate.

For the sauce: Add the preserves and water to a small saucepan. Bring to a simmer, stirring; turn off. Strain if desired.

To cook the crêpes: Place an 8-inch nonstick skillet over medium heat; spray lightly with vegetable oil. Pour ¼ cup of batter into the center of the pan and tilt it around so the batter covers the bottom evenly. Cook for about 1 minute then flip with a spatula and cook the other side for 30 seconds. Transfer the crêpes to a plate, and continue until the batter is gone.

To make the blintzes: Spoon 2 tablespoon of the filling into the center bottom third of a crêpe. Fold the bottom up over the filling, fold in the sides, and roll to make a neat package.

When all the blintzes are filled, melt the butter in a nonstick skillet. Brown the blintzes lightly on each side, starting with the seal side down. Transfer them to a lightly buttered baking dish. Bake for 15 minutes. Let rest for 5 minutes before serving with the fruit sauce. Dust with confectioners' sugar, if desired.

banana nut bread

Next time those bananas are looking a little past their prime, remember this great nutty loaf.

serves 6

2 cups all-purpose flour

1 teaspoon salt

1 teaspoon baking powder

1 teaspoon baking soda

½ cup (1 stick) unsalted butter, softened

1 cup sugar

2 large eggs

1½ cups mashed banana (usually 3 bananas is perfect)

1 cup chopped walnuts

2 tablespoons milk

Preheat oven to 325°F. Whisk together the flour, salt, baking powder, and baking soda in a mixing bowl for one minute; reserve until needed.

Cream the butter and sugar together until light and fluffy. Beat in the eggs one at a time, mixing thoroughly before adding the next. Mix in the bananas, walnuts, and milk until combined. Add the flour mixture, stirring just until combined.

Pour batter into a buttered and lightly-floured 9 x 5-inch loaf pan. Bake for about 1 hour and 10 minutes, or until a tester inserted in the center comes out clean. Let cool 20 minutes before removing from the pan.

buttermilk biscuits

Making buttermilk biscuits would be the first event in any American food decathlon. Anyone can make them, but to get great biscuits it helps to have a gentle and intuitive disposition. Use a light touch because over-mixing will toughen the dough.

makes 12-14

2 cups all-purpose flour

2 teaspoons baking powder

¼ teaspoon baking soda

1 teaspoon salt

7 tablespoons unsalted butter, cut into thin slices, chilled in freezer

¾ cup cold buttermilk

Preheat oven to 425°F. In a mixing bowl, whisk together the dry ingredients to thoroughly combine. Cut in the ice cold butter slices using a wire pastry blender, until the mixture has the texture of coarse crumbs.

Make a well in the center and pour in the cold buttermilk. Stir the dry ingredients into the buttermilk with a fork until a loose, sticky dough is formed. Stop as soon as the mixture comes together. Form into a ball and turn the dough out onto a floured work surface.

With floured hands, pat the dough into a rectangle (about 8 x 4-inch-thick). Fold dough in thirds (like folding a letter-sized piece of paper). Repeat this process twice more.

On a lightly-floured surface, roll or pat the dough out about ½-inch thick. Cut with a round biscuit cutter, and place on a parchment or silicon mat-lined baking sheet, a few inches apart. You can gather up any extra dough after cutting, and repeat to get a few more biscuits, although the texture may suffer from the extra working.

Make a slight depression in the center of each biscuit with your thumb (to help them rise evenly). Brush the tops lightly with buttermilk. Bake for about 15 minutes, or until risen and golden brown. Cool on a rack for 10 minutes before serving.

index

muffins
    blueberry muffins 42
    double chocolate muffins 46
    lemon poppy seed muffins 40

new orleans-style french toast 86
new york cheesecake with fruit sauce 74
nuts
    banana nut bread 90
    butterscotch blondies 18
    carrot cake with cream cheese frosting 34
    chocolate and oat bars 22
    chocolate chip cookies 8
    chocolate walnut fudge 12
    cinnamon swirl sour cream bundt cake 38
    double fudge brownies 14
    peanut butter cookies 10
    pecan pie 58
    pumpkin crumb cake 48

oats
    chocolate and oat bars 22
    cinnamon raisin bars 20
    pumpkin crumb cake 48
    very berry crisp 72
    oranges
    new york cheesecake with fruit sauce 74
    pound cake with orange glaze 32
    rhubarb crumble 78

peach cobbler 80
peanut butter cookies 10
pecans
    carrot cake with cream cheese frosting 34
    pecan pie 58
pies
    apple pie 52
    blueberry pie 60
    cherry pie 62
    lemon meringue pie 56
    mississippi mud pie 64
    pecan pie 58
    sweet potato pie 54
pineapple: carrot cake with cream cheese frosting 34
pound cake with orange glaze 32
pumpkin crumb cake 48
pumpkin sandwich cake 28

raisins
    bread and butter pudding with whiskey sauce 76

cinnamon raisin bars 20
red velvet cake 30
rhubarb crumble 78
sweet potato pie 54

vanilla hearts 24
vanilla ice cream with chocolate sauce 68

walnuts
    banana nut bread 90
    carrot cake with cream cheese frosting 34
    chocolate chip cookies 8
    chocolate walnut fudge 12
    cinnamon swirl sour cream bundt cake 38
    double fudge brownies 14
    pumpkin crumb cake 48
    whoopie pies 44